D0980133

David Budbill

Happy Life

COPPER CANYON PRESS
Port Townsend, Washington

Copyright 2011 by David Budbill

All rights reserved

Printed in the United States of America

Cover art: *Six Improvisations in Black and Red III*, 10 × 10 inches, ink and acrylic (2009) and *Six Improvisations in Black and Red V*, 10 × 10 inches, ink and acrylic (2009), by Lois Eby, photographed by Paul Rogers Photography

Copper Canyon Press is in residence at Fort Worden State Park in Port Townsend, Washington, under the auspices of Centrum. Centrum is a gathering place for artists and creative thinkers from around the world, students of all ages and backgrounds, and audiences seeking extraordinary cultural enrichment.

LIBRARY OF CONGRESS
CATALOGING-IN-PUBLICATION DATA

Budbill, David.
Happy life / David Budbill.
   p. cm.
ISBN 978-1-55659-374-1 (alk. paper)
I. Title.
PS3552.U346H37 2011
811´.54—dc22

                                          2011010988

9 8 7 6 5 4 3 2   FIRST PRINTING

COPPER CANYON PRESS
Post Office Box 271
Port Townsend, Washington 98368
www.coppercanyonpress.org

HAPPY LIFE

Books by David Budbill

POEMS

Happy Life
Drink a Cup of Loneliness
While We've Still Got Feet
Moment to Moment: Poems of a Mountain Recluse
Judevine: The Complete Poems
Why I Came to Judevine
From Down to the Village
The Chain Saw Dance
Barking Dog

SHORT STORIES

Snowshoe Trek to Otter River

NOVEL

The Bones on Black Spruce Mountain

CHILDREN'S BOOK

Christmas Tree Farm

EDITED VOLUME

Danvis Tales: Selected Stories by Rowland E. Robinson

For more information about all of these works
go to www.davidbudbill.com

for Lois
    45 years

ACKNOWLEDGMENTS

Grateful acknowledgment to the books and magazines in
which some of these poems first appeared: *bottle rockets, The
Café Review, Entelechy International, Exterminating Angel
Press, Green Living, Nine Taoist Poems, The Poet's Cookbook,
The Salon, Seven Days, Silent Solos: Improvisers Speak,
Turning Wheel, Vermont Life.*

Reading other poets' poems inspired many of the poems in
this book. The ancient Chinese poets called making poems
this way "harmonization." Here is a very partial list of poets
and translators to whom I am indebted for nearly forty years
of inspiration: Han Shan, Burton Watson, Arthur Tobias,
Gary Snyder, Shōtetsu, Steven D. Carter, Yang Wan-li, Jonathan
Chaves, Stonehouse, Bill Porter, Baisaō, Norman Waddell,
Steve Sanfield, Olav H. Hauge, Robert Bly, Robert Hedin,
Robin Fulton, Chia Tao, Mike O'Connor, Emily Dickinson,
Bashō, Cid Corman, Kamaike Susumu, Po Chü-i, David
Hinton, Wang Wei, Chang Yin-nan, Lewis C. Walmsley, Lao
Tzu, Gia-fu Feng, Jane English, Daisetz T. Suzuki, Leonard
Koren, J.P. Seaton, Dennis Maloney, C.H. Kwock, Vincent
McHugh, Paul Reps, David Young, Meng Hao-jan, Ryōkan,
John Stevens, Nobuyuki Yuasa, Ono no Komachi, Izumi
Shikibu, Jane Hirshfield, Mariko Aratani, Yuan Mei, to name
just a few.

Monks and nuns who live in the mountains
don't have to register with anyone.

HSU-TUNG

Anyone comes here looking for
the "special transmission" of Zen
I'll point them under their noses
to matters of their everyday life.

BAISAŌ

Contents

PART THREE

HAPPY LIFE

Part One

·

Chia Tao Begins a Poem to Subprefect Li K'uo of Hu County by Saying

I can't help feeling for you—
leaving your office work
only to meet each time
the dying day.

I've spent most of my life
pissing and moaning about
never having any money,
not being known, never
getting any honors, not
getting to travel.

And yet,
for more than forty years
my days have been my own.

It takes a long time for some people
to realize how lucky they are.

Just Silence and Stillness

this warm September morning.
    No wind, no birds' songs,
no jets going over
    at 30,000 feet,

but later today the wind will pick up,
    a slight breeze begin.
A pileated woodpecker will call
    off in the woods somewhere.

Ravens will begin their croaking
    over near the Ledges.
Chickadees and nuthatches
    will fuss in the yard.

I'll pick up my bamboo flute
    and join them.
But just now, none of that, just now,
    silence and stillness,

a quiet, so profound I think
    I can hear my own heart beating.

Upside Down

All the plants that on the deck this summer
gave us so much pleasure: upside down now
on the compost pile: going back to where
they came from:

petunia, salvia, begonia, geranium, pansy,
fuchsia, and that volunteer tomato that came up
out of the compost in the petunia pot, grew,
blossomed and bore fruit among all those flowers.

All that color, all that joy and light:
gone back now to darkness, back to rot,
to make fertility, fecundity, fruitfulness
for next year.

Tomatoes in September

Every surface in the house covered
    with tomatoes, a vat
of boiling water on the stove,
    drop them in and wait for
cracks in their skins. Into cold water. Out.
    Cut away the bad spots,
cut out stem end and blossom end,
    peel away the skin,
chop them up, drain them in a colander—
    save the juice to drink—
dump them into the other
    pot in which a mountain of garlic
has been simmering in olive oil:
    Brandywine, Juliet, Cosmonaut,
Rose de Berne, all go in,
    salt and pepper,
basil, thyme, oregano,
    then
let it bubble
    while you
go smell
    the house.

Everything

after 9/11/2001

Milkweed pods
crack open
seeds dishevel
fall

Everything
sweeter and
more fragile
now

September Visitors

I'm glad to see our friends come:
talk, laughter, food, wine.
I'm glad to see our friends go:
solitude, emptiness, gardens,
autumn wind.

A Certain Slant of Light

A certain slant
of light

this time of year
says more than

color in the hills
or chill air

that fall
is here.

The Full September Moon

Moonlight shimmers, turning
wheat blossoms into snow
PO CHÜ-I

I woke in the middle of the night
and beyond the window

snow on the ground and on
the branches of the white pine tree

For a moment I didn't know
what month it was

The full September moon
shone white upon the lawn

Sometimes

When day after day we have cloudless blue skies,
warm temperatures, colorful trees, and brilliant sun, when
it seems like all this will go on forever,

when I harvest vegetables from the garden all day,
then drink tea and doze in the late afternoon sun,
and in the evening one night make pickled beets
and green tomato chutney, the next night
red tomato chutney, and the day after that
pick the fruits of my arbor and make grape jam,

when we walk in the woods every evening over fallen leaves,
through yellow light, when nights are cool, and days warm,

when I am so happy I am afraid I might explode or disappear
or somehow be taken away from all this,

at those times when I feel so happy, so good, so alive, so in love
with the world, with my own sensuous, beautiful life, suddenly

I think about all the suffering and pain in the world, about
all those people being tortured, right now, in my name. But
I still feel happy and good, alive and in love with the world
and with my lucky, guilty, sensuous, beautiful life, because

I know in the next minute or tomorrow all this may be taken from me,
and therefore I've got to say, right now, what I feel and know and see,
I've got to say, right now, how beautiful and sweet this world can be.

Out in the Woods

The only time I'm really free is when I'm out in the woods
cutting firewood, stacking brush, clearing trails.

Just the chain saw, the dog, and me.
Heave and groan, sweat and ache.

Work until I can't stand it anymore.
Take a break.

Sit on the needle-strewn ground up against a big pine tree,
drink some water, stare out through the woods, pet the dog.

Stretch out on the ground, take a nap,
dog's head on my lap.

Ah, this would be the time and place and way
to die.

Mid-October

Almost all the leaves
are down. Rain.

Clouds make a fog
just above the trees.

The world colder
more empty every day.

My favorite
time of year.

October 17

All day I worked outside in the cold air
under a heavy sky, running a chain saw,

stacking firewood, tearing up the last bits
of garden, turning compost. Now outside

a cold wind blows, a cold rain
comes down. Inside, I lie under a quilt,

drinking sweet black tea and warm milk
and reading poems from long ago.

Now

Now the crickets come inside
    and sing upon the hearth.

They say, *Oh! Oh! Autumn*
    is coming to an end.

They say, *Oh! Winter*
    is just around the bend.

They say, *Oh! Oh!*
    The year is dying.

They say, *Oh!*
    We are dying, too.

They say, *Oh! Oh!*
    So are you!

Forty Years Ago

Forty years ago I had an urge to go away from the world,
retreat, into the mountains. At that time I had little idea this
kind of thing was part of an ancient tradition. I knew nothing
about Taoist Chinese hermits; I'd read few ancient Chinese poems.

All I knew was: I couldn't stand where or who I was anymore.
I was only twenty-nine. Yet the vision was distinct and undeniable.
I turned my back on all kinds of possibilities, opportunities, ambitions,
not to mention disastrous scenarios, for the rest of my life.

I went away instead into anonymity. I went to work in the woods,
a common laborer among other common laborers—just like all
my relatives had been back there in Cleveland.

I felt at home among these people and in my new mountain home.

Happiness

In ancient times a rabbi went around saying, *Where is it written that we should be happy?* In more recent times the Declaration of Independence said happiness is something we have the right to pursue. It says nothing about how or whether we can catch it.

Life and Liberty are the only rights we've got, the Declaration of Independence says. Happiness we just get the right to chase. So go ahead already—chase it if you want to. But before you go, here's a tip from old Yang Wan-li, who said,

When I pursue happiness, I can never find it. Then suddenly when I'm not looking it just appears.

Last Day of October

Last day of October.
Toward evening.
Woods quiet.
Birds gone.

Only the dog and I
on the logging road
moving slowly over
wet leaves.

A Long and Gracious Fall

This collection of verses... portrays in accurate detail the circumstances of his daily life.

DAICHŌ RŌRYŌ, WRITING ABOUT HIS DHARMA
BROTHER, BAISAŌ

A long and gracious fall this year.
The leaves are down. Gardens: emptied,
manured, tilled, smooth, and waiting.
Mower and tiller serviced and put away.

Smoker put away, as is the summer table.
Prayer flags, windsocks and their poles: down.
Twenty-foot homemade badminton poles,
peace flag at the top of one, store-bought net—
all down and put away for another year. No more
outdoor summer chores.

Fall planting—peonies and tiger lilies—done.
Summer flower stalks removed, beds mulched,
a blanket for the cold. Fall pruning done.

Woodshed roof hammered down and sealed again.
Cellar closed. Drive staked and flagged so the
snowplow knows where to go.

What else is there to do? Finally, for once, we are ready
for the snow. Ready now to come inside. Time now for
words and music, poems and shakuhachi. Time now
to light some incense, sit and stare at candlelight.

The Fall Almost Nobody Sees

Everybody's gone away.
They think there's nothing left to see.
The garish colors' flashy show is over.
Now those of us who stay
hunker down in sweet silence,
blessed emptiness among

red-orange shadblow
purple-red blueberry
copper-brown beech
gold tamarack, a few
remaining pale yellow
popple leaves,
sedge and fern in shades
from beige to darkening red
to brown to almost black,
and all this in front of, below,
among blue-green spruce and fir
and white pine,

all of it under gray skies,
chill air, all of us waiting
in the somber dank and rain,
waiting here in quiet, chill
November,
waiting for the snow.

Come Inside Now

Come inside now.
Stand beside the warming stove.
Watch out through the windows as
a cold rain tears down
the last leaves.

The larder full of dried herbs,
hot peppers, chutneys,
jellies, jams, dill pickles,
pickled relishes,
pickled beets.

The freezer full of frozen greens—
chard and spinach, collards, kale—
green beans, basil, red sauces,
applesauce, and
smoked meats.

The woodshed dry and full of wood,
winter squashes stashed away.
Down cellar: potatoes, carrots,
crock of sauerkraut.

Come inside now.
Stand beside the warming stove.
Listen. Wait.

Part Two

First Thing in the Morning

Slate-colored
junco tracks
on the porch

printed neatly
in the
thin snow

My Punishment

I get up before the sun,
make a fire in the woodstove,
boil water, make tea,
watch the dawn come.
Then I get back in bed,
under the quilt,
propped up on my pillows,
read a little, drink my tea
and stare out the window
at the snow coming down.

Oh, this lazybones life!

Others rush off to work while
I lie here in silence waiting for
a few words to come drifting
over from the Other Side.
No wonder I never make any
money. I am being punished
for having such a good time.

Cold Winter Night

Fire going in the Round Oak
greased boots glistening
behind the stove

Pull a chair up close
little glass of whiskey
book of ancient poems

.

Some Good Advice from a Friend, or
On Not Being Awarded a Poetry Prize, Again

for Joseph Bednarik

Well, we all get caught up, from time to time,
    in the temptations of this world.
Sometimes we think about prestige, book sales,
    notoriety, even for something as
lowly and insignificant as a prize
    for being a poet.

We all need, from time to time, a friend
    to tell us, as a friend told me,
This is, truly, a relief, because
    reincarnated Chinese poets should
worry only about their gardens and where
    their next poem might be coming from.

Weed the beans. Pick the peas.
Hill the potatoes. Thin the chard.
Cut more wood.

Contradictions

Lao Tzu said, *Beautiful words are not true.*
True words are not beautiful. I think
what Lao Tzu really meant to say was,
No words are best.

Po Chü-i wrote ten thousand poems
and every day cursed his poetry karma
as he sought the Silence of the Way.

Poor Po Chü-i, every day, brushing out
another poem and swearing at himself
for doing it.

Who we are and who
we want to be
are so seldom the same.

Chiho's Calligraphy

for Chiho Kaneko

Chiho brushed for me
three Chinese characters.
She sent them to me in the mail.

I have her calligraphy framed on the wall
in my room above my little homemade
altar where I sit every day.

The characters from top to bottom say:
Shu, which means keep or obey,
as in obey the teacher.

The second one is *ha*, which means
break, rebel, try things out, other than
what the teacher said.

The third one is *ri*, which means
depart on your own path,
go your own way.

Into the Winter Woods

Long-johns top and bottom, heavy socks, flannel shirt, overalls,
steel-toed work boots, sweater, canvas coat, toque, mittens: on.

Out past grape arbor and garden shed, into the woods.
Sun just coming through the trees. There really *is* such a thing

as Homer's *rosy-fingered dawn.* And here it is, this morning.
Down hill, across brook, up hill, and into the stand of white pine

and red maple where I'm cutting firewood. Open up workbox,
take out chain saw, gas, bar oil, kneel down, gas up saw, add

bar oil to the reservoir, stand up, mittens off, strap on and buckle
chaps from waist to toe, hard hat helmet: on. Ear protectors: down,

face screen: down, push in compression release, pull out choke,
pull on starter cord, once, twice, go. Stall. Pull out choke, pull on

starter cord, once, twice, go. Push in choke. Mittens: back on.
Cloud of two-cycle exhaust smoke wafting into the morning air

and I, looking like a medieval Japanese warrior, wade through
blue smoke, knee-deep snow, revving the chain saw as I go,

headed for that doomed, unknowing maple tree.

On Looking at a Picture of Myself

Who is that old guy standing in front of my woodpile?
How come he's got my overalls and chaps and my
hard hat on? And he's wearing my mittens, too. And
that's my chain saw on top the woodpile just behind him.

He looks just like my father, exactly like my father.
Where did he come from? What's he doing there?

He does a nice job though. I can see that from here.
The firewood is evenly cut and carefully and evenly
stacked. And I can also see he stacks his brush
carefully, too. He does a lot better job than I did

when I was young. Maybe I ought to try to track
him down and see if he would like to work with
me out in the woods. He does a nice job, even if
he is an old guy and looks just like my father.

Ode to Wood

Too long have I not sung the praises
    of our hardwood trees,
felled, cut, stacked, dried, and hauled
    to the house and woodshed,
then split and brought inside all winter long
    to put inside our woodstove,
to burn, to keep us warm. This wood
    that grows less than half a mile
from our house, these trees
    that grow faster than I
can cut them down,
    always making more
than we can use.

Oh, finally I sing the praises of wood.
    Homegrown and handy, abundant,
convenient, cheap, the growth of these hills
    right here at home.

Finally now, I sing the praises
    of our hardwood trees.

Ode to Our Woodstove

Inside this little wooden house
        on a Vermont slate hearth
stands our trusty, faithful, large
        and sturdy, cast-iron stove
in which for more than forty years
        I have built from fall to summer
fire after fire
        to keep us warm.

Oh, to get up on a cold winter morning,
        start the tea water, then make
a fire and while the tea steeps, add some
        logs to what's already going,
then stand beside the big old stove,
        and feel the warmth
radiating out from its cast iron into
        the room and me, while I drink
my tea and daydream,
        watching out the window.

O, Round Oak stove made by the Estate
        of P.D. Beckwith in Dowagiac,
Michigan, more than 100 years ago,
        finally, now I sing your praises.
I praise your great gift to us
        over all these years.

Ode to Fire, Ode to Heat

a mountain recluse doesn't have many plans
all he talks about is his fire
STONEHOUSE

Half my wintertime life, or so it seems,
    I spend standing beside our old
wood-burning stove—which stands at the center
    of our house—hands behind my back,
resting on my butt, palms out, warmth
    of the fire in the woodstove working its
way into my body. Then turn around and
    bake the other side. Too hot? Just move
a step or two away. It's so simple, easy.
    And all you've got to do is work
all year, sweat and heave and groan
    to make this little moment happen.

Now I praise primordial fire, I praise
    heat in its most basic form:
this blessed warmth that comes from our old,
    wood-burning Round Oak stove.

Now I sing the praises of a wood fire,
    of the heat this smoky burning liberates,
this dry heat that keeps us warm all winter,
    even when it's 35 below.

Contrasts

Off to the City.
Everything so different,
one place from the other.

Crowded and noisy streets
of the City, the solitude of
the quiet mountainside:

human-nonhuman, hectic-
calm, bright-dark, yang-yin.
The sages say it's all the same.

I don't know; they sure seem
different to me. Each magnifies,
is better with, the other.

Written After Seeing an East Asian Miniature from an Illustrated Manuscript in a Display at the Metropolitan Museum of Art in New York City and Then Thinking about Vice President Dick Cheney

In 16th-century Lahore the artist Miskin, on the leaf of a manuscript, depicted the story of how the King one day while hunting in the countryside shot a bird with his bow and arrow. When the King approached the bird, he discovered, much to his dismay, that the bird was, in fact, a young man, who lay now lifeless on the ground with an arrow through his chest. Overcome with grief at what he had done, the King approached the young man's mother, who was sobbing nearby. The King called his servants to bring forth two golden bowls and place them on the ground between himself and the bereaved woman. The King then spoke to the grieving mother, saying *In order to make amends for my grievous error, I offer you a choice. In one of these golden bowls you may have as much gold coinage of the realm as the bowl will hold, or, in the other, you may have my head. The choice is yours.* When the King was done speaking, he called his servants forth with bags of gold enough to fill to overflowing one of the golden bowls. Then the King drew his sword and handed it to a servant, rolled his collar down, knelt, bowed his head, and prepared to die. Here there was a pause of quite some time while the King waited for the mother's decision. At last, the mother of the young man, knowing that revenge is futile, accepted the golden bowl filled with gold to overflowing. Upon departing, the mother, through her tears, exhorted the King to continue his just rule. Thus the mother and the King went their separate ways, each carrying their own grief from that place.

Cynical Capitalists

Privatize profit.
Socialize loss.

Three Days in New York: A Blues in B$^\flat$

for William Parker

I

At the Painting Center on Greene Street surrounded by Ying Li's paintings,
oil and acrylic on canvas, of rivers and mountains and sky, fields in
    the distance
and apple trees—all only vaguely there in these thickly painted,
    abstract, and
intense splashes of color exploding off the canvas, emotion-laden strokes
of the brush growing out of her life with Chinese calligraphy—all here on
    these
canvases, this so-called Western, so-called European art.

II

The New Chao Chow Restaurant on Mott a block above Canal:
        Water Cress in Bean Curd Sauce
        Steamed Whole Flounder smothered in shredded scallions
            and ginger
        Seafood Hot Pot
        Duck
And for dessert a turn around the corner to the Italian bakery
    on Mulberry,
the one right next to the Luna. Then out again and walkin', eatin' cannolis
on Canal Street headed for the Q train.

III

On the balcony overlooking the Rotunda at the Metropolitan Museum
    of Art
a display of pottery showing how the ancient Chinese and Persian empires

(Iran and Iraq) influenced each other, how Buddhist, Taoist, and
    Muslim potters
traded back and forth ideas for glazes, colors, designs, shapes for
    their vessels—
all this back and forth on the Silk Road and Steppe Route thousands of
    years ago.
Who told us Europe discovered the world?

IV

155th Street and Frederick Douglass Boulevard, Charles' Southern
    Style Kitchen:
        Collard Greens
        Fried Chicken
        Spare Ribs in Barbecue Sauce
        Collard Greens
        Macaroni and Cheese
        Chicken in Barbecue Sauce
        Collard Greens
        Corn Bread
        Collard Greens
and your choice of Lemonade or Sweet Iced Tea.

V

There are shards of 12th-century Chinese celadon pottery on the
    beaches of
East Africa. The Chinese were there with whole armies and horses, gobs
of stuff centuries before the European colonizers ever dreamed of
    going there.
Who told us Europe discovered the world?

VI

Polyglot   Gumbo   Masala   Stew
Hybrids   Bastards   Mutts   All of us
All sloshed together   Ain't it grand?

VII

And here I am this old white guy all decked out in my
yellow, orange, red, black, blue, and white dashiki
and my blue and gold African mirror hat playing
Japanese bamboo flute and ropes of bells from India
and a gong from Tibet, with these far-out, crazy
jazz musicians what come in how many different
shades of flesh and nationality, and me right here
on the Lower East Side in New York City reading my
cracker, woodchuck, honky, ofay, green mountains,
ersatz Chinese, wilderness poetry.

Three Lines for the End of February

Snow continues to deepen.
Seed order's in.
Days noticeably longer.

That Night

Finally now, down at the bottom of the hill, near the brook,
    in the bottomland in the swampy place
    among the alders—nothing left.

Raven tracks everywhere. Over here two hind legs joined together
    by some hide, over there the forelegs
    scattered about, and in between, as if it were the

centerpiece for the dining room table: ribcage, spine,
    and skull, all picked clean, nothing left, only a little
    red flesh clinging to ribs, jaw, eye socket, vertebrae,

the bloody snow packed down by tracks of dog, coyote,
    turkey, raven, bear, blue jay, fisher, raccoon, bobcat:
    the whole forest come to dine.

Part Three

Here at the Birth of Spring

How many more times
around this wheel for me?

Why would my melancholy
overwhelm me now,

here, at the birth of spring?

Sleep and I Are Strangers

Yang Wan-li said, *The night is long. Sleep is sweet.*
The poet's thoughts are bitter. I cannot fall asleep.
I wonder if I will ever sleep again. 800 years later

I say—Sometimes I see her on the street. Our eyes
meet—hers seem to say, *Tonight I will come home*
with you, climb into your bed, wrap myself around you,

love you, lull you, and then together we will sleep.
But she casts her eyes away, and passes by down
the street, and I am left alone again, wandering

the night, wide eyed, awake, wondering
when I might see her again.

Sweet Early Spring

When the understory of the woods
        is flattened
and you can see the contours
        of the earth,
the rock outcroppings—all this
        just after the
last pockets of snow disappear,
        while everything
is still sere, brown, gray—when
        now and then
a woodcock whistles or you can hear
        a lone goose
going somewhere—all this, this sweet
        early spring—
with no bugs at all, none, not a single one—
        this
clear, beautiful, and brief moment,
        this emptiness—
this is the time
        I love the best—
before the world fills up again with
        insects, leaves,
brush, birds, green: a last brief rest—
        quiet and peace—
before I have to turn and face
        the lush and fertile
noisy spring.

The Heart of Evening

for Gene Wolf Budbill
1967–2007

Day over. Wind gone.
No sound but
an owl far away.

Let my careworn heart
take refuge
in the heart of evening.

Late April

Crocuses gone by
Daffodils in bloom
Peonies poking through
Grass just now turning green
Warblers in the naked apple tree
Woodcock whistle 'n' *peent*
Two geese nesting in the swamp
Black ants in the kitchen

Spring again this year

This Morning

Oh, this life,
the now,
this morning,

which I
can turn
into forever

by simply
loving
what is here,

is gone
by noon.

Apple Blossoms

Apple blossoms
swell and bloom
and fall.

No one can
escape
old age.

Little Poem Written at Five O'Clock in the Morning

All this violence: wars and cruelties—
collective and individual—
carnage of all kinds,
now as always
back to the beginning of time.

Our kind endlessly slaughters itself;
our appetite for self-destruction is boundless.

Yet and still every day the sun rises,
white clouds roll across the sky,
vegetables get planted and grow,
and late in the afternoon someone
sits quietly with a cup of tea.

A Day Off

It's been the usual frantic spring:
      prune the apple trees, till the gardens,
turn the compost, work on the new shed,
      do the first mowings, plant
the early vegetables, set out the hardy seedlings:
      one thing after another,
day after day, no time for flutes or books,
      only time to be outdoors and
nothing but work, work, work,
      work, work, work,

until, that is, I hurt my foot and now
      I'm so lame I can barely stand,
which means, I have to spend the day in bed
      with tea, the history of
Sung Dynasty poetry and the life of Yang Wan-li—
      showing once again how
misfortune
      sometimes brings its opposite.

May: The Pond Is Full

Always too poor to dig the pond. For forty years the pond site
has remained only a wet place waiting to become something else.

Only in my imagination do I see an acre of water and just
beyond a wood duck nest at the edge of the limitless trees, and

in the pond, brook trout dimple the surface, channel cats poke
along the bottom; only in my imagination do I see myself cooking

catfish and trout smothered in slivers of scallions and ginger, then
tamari splashed across them popping in the wok's hot oil and out

onto the platter. Only in my imagination do I see myself floating
in a boat or swimming among caddisfly, dragonfly, mayfly, or

sitting on the bank watching the water, knowing an inner calm
as peaceful, as still, as the quiet water. All this: only in a dream.

Morning Schedule: Early May

Cat gets me up at 4:30.
Wants to go out. Back to
bed till 5:00, can't sleep,
might as well get up.

Make tea, get back in bed,
read some ancient Chinese
poems, maybe write a poem
myself. Up again at 6:00.

Fry two eggs, toast a big hunk
of rye, butter, jam. Get dressed
for the woods, overalls, boots,
gloves, and so on. Head out in

the early morning light: 7:00.
Chilly, in the 30s. Drop some
trees, stack brush, stack blocks
of wood, a couple of hours.

See Spring Beauty on my way home.
Five little petals in a whorl white and
purple stripèd: brilliant pink. Five
filaments with purple anthers in a

perfect circle. Nothing fearful about
this symmetry. O, little almost-not-
there beauty, hello sweet flower.
Welcome back.

Another Day

Early May, the trees just coming into leaf,
spinach and peas, five kinds of lettuce
already in the ground and up, but still
too cold to plant anything else. Back out
to the woods, put bug dope on and cut
more wood. Late afternoon, the sun not
yet going down, yet I, bone sore and aching,
head home through the yellow light. Stop
at the brook, stand and watch and listen.
Light through evergreens makes a dappled,
rattling quietude of irresistible tranquillity.
Walking easy now, home.

Off with my overalls and shirt, boots and socks,
that sweet smell of gas, oil, and fresh-cut wood.
Crack some ice cubes in a glass, couple of twists
of lemon peel and Scotch. Sit out on the deck in
my underwear, let this alcohol ease my aching
body, here in the evening chill, this easy breeze,
watch the dying light, while way down inside
my lucky self, I sing praises for another day.

A Land of Such Beauty

Po Chü-i says, *It's a land of such beauty.*
There's never been lord or master here.
Mountain realms are themselves. And,
I would add, so are the people who live there.

It's funny. My Old Pal—whom I've never met
and who's never been here—because he's
been dead for 1,200 years—knows exactly
what it's like here on Judevine Mountain.

My Teacher

*I laid my heart open to the benign
indifference of the universe*
ALBERT CAMUS

Nature is my teacher.

She never asks me anything,
never says a word.

In her class: no assignments,
deadlines, or requirements.

Benign, indifferent,
she doesn't care what I do.

All she does is wait.

You Ask Me Why

Li Po said,
You ask why I live
in these green mountains.

I got stuck here.
Too poor to move,
maybe too afraid to,
didn't want to anyway,
thought maybe
there might be
something worthwhile here
someday,
if I could
stick it out.

That was forty years ago.

Call Ahead

If you come here
for a visit,
please,
call ahead.

But if you just show up,
don't be offended
if
I'm not here.

I may be out in the woods
putting up my firewood,
or
maybe

I'm just hiding,
wanting to stay
alone
in this place.

Fake Hermit

I'm not the mountain recluse I pretend to be.
I've got a wife who's been here with me for more
than forty years, and a grown daughter

who lives just down the road, a dead son, and
we've got lots of friends around here, too.
I'm not the hermit I pretend to be.

On the other hand, I bet I get fewer visitors
than all those Chinese hermits in the mountains
long ago. They had people coming by all the time

just to see the one who leads such a different life.
At least I'm spared that constant string of visitors.
Don't get me wrong. I like my life this way: mostly,

but not entirely, alone. Like today: I love a day
like today when I can spend all day wandering
through the woods and my imagination, all alone.

Words to Live By

Lu-ch'iu Yin, like all good Taoists and Buddhists, sought wisdom and enlightenment. Lu had heard there were two bodhisattvas whose names were Cold Mountain and Pickup living as paupers and lunatics in the mountains not far from

Taichou where Lu was governor. Lu sent a magistrate to find out if the stories about Cold Mountain and Pickup were true. When word came back that indeed there were two men with those names who fit that description, Lu-ch'iu Yin himself

made a pilgrimage to find the two and pay his respects. Upon arriving at Kuoching, the temple where Cold Mountain and Pickup were supposed to be, Lu asked the monks where he could find two poverty-stricken lunatics. The monks led Lu

to the kitchen where he saw two servants, rough and ignorant-looking men, standing by the stove laughing. When Lu-ch'iu Yin saw the two, Lu prostrated himself on the kitchen floor. The two bodhisattvas seeing this both screamed and ran out

of the kitchen laughing. The monks pursued the kitchen help, but the two crazies were fast runners and they got away. Thus it was that Lu-ch'iu Yin, governor of Taichou, did not get his chance to worship at the feet of Cold Mountain and Pickup.

Two Places

for Steve Sanfield

Steve and I both, in 1969,
fled the world of Red Dust.

He to Northern California,
I to northern Vermont.

We both built places
away from anywhere.

He on the Ridge near the
South Fork of the Yuba River,

I on the western slopes
of Judevine Mountain.

Both of us equidistant
from our separate oceans,

separated by America, both
determined to find some other

way to live our lives, and
leave America between us.

After Too Much Traveling

Back home now on my quiet mountainside
among my gardens and woods,

vegetables sprouting, firewood stacked and covered,
wildflowers blooming, trees coming into leaf,

bird songs, black flies
spring again, and home.

Sunday Morning

Our neighbor's home-cured, applewood-smoked, slab bacon
I've sliced myself. Mary Jo's cage-free organic eggs "the girls"

have made for us. Two for each of us, one for Lu Shan, our dog.
And sometimes my own homegrown potatoes parboiled and fried

in oil with onions, green pepper, celery, herb salt, and black pepper.
A little stack of toast from bread baked locally and spread with local

butter. Three or four kinds of jam, one of which I made myself from
my own grapes. A pot of tea—Keemun or Assam, a little golden Yunnan

tossed in. Then sit down at the table as the early morning sun
comes streaming through the windows.

Question and Answer

after Li Po

You ask me
why I live on
this green mountain.

I smile: no answer.

Come.
Live here
forty years.

You'll see.

I Hate to See the Trees Leaf Out

I like spring warmth, the birds' return,
all that sensuous summer heat,

but I also hate to see the trees leaf out,
the world fill up, this summer glut of green.

All that lovely, empty barrenness
of late winter, early spring,

gone.

Early June

Hard rain all night
morning rags of mist
hang scattered
between the
blue-green hills

Part Four

Sex and Ambition

Sometimes I leave this mountain home and go to
  the City
where I see young and beautiful women everywhere,
  all of them
preoccupied with sex and ambition, none of them
  able to imagine
themselves
  white-haired, wizened, bent, and sore.

And I, approaching my own old age, beginning to
  know myself
as white-haired, wizened, bent, and sore,
  I am—
I am happy to say—I am still, like those
  young women,
preoccupied
  with sex and ambition.

Finally, Now

If I hadn't been consumed by ambition
for all those years I wouldn't know
how much ambition alters everything.

But finally, now, I'm old enough
to understand, and therefore
I'm not in such a hurry anymore.

I take my time. I load the woodshed
carefully and slow. I thin the lettuces
and spinach with greater delicacy now.

And there are other benefits to growing
old. You all, of course, remember
that old blues line that goes:

Chicks don't like it when you
take it fast so take it slow
and make it last.

I'm slowing down in lots
of ways. I don't run from
one thing to another anymore.

What's the hurry? I'm
slowing down so I can be
late for my own funeral.

Please, Buddha

In my middle age
I used to say,
Buddha, please,
save me
from my lust.

Now I'm over seventy
and I say,
Please, Buddha,
never
save me from my lust.

Wilderness in the City

Here I am, the mountain recluse, in the City again.

I turn the corner on Avenue A
and head east on Sixth Street toward Avenue B.
Then
barreling down the street two stories off the ground
between rows of five-story walk-ups
comes a peregrine falcon,
a pigeon flapping from her right talons.

The falcon banks to the right,
heads for the second-story landing of a fire escape,
settles in, and has her lunch.

The people passing by, completely consumed by their lives,
ideas, careers, passions, obsessions, ambitions,
plunge down the street—
blood drips on their heads,
the air snows feathers—
all of them oblivious to what is going on
fifteen feet above them.

For forty years I've lived a solitary life
in the wild and lonely mountains seven hours north of here
and never have I seen
anything like this.

The Subway Philanthropist

for George W. Bush

The Emperor of Death loves only weapons and money and
so long as he is on the throne, the Subway Philanthropist
plies his trade, prowling the bowels of New York City moving
deliberately from subway station to subway station dropping
fifty-dollar bills into white plastic five-gallon buckets, saxo-
phone cases, violin cases, upturned straw hats, Tupperware
bowls, all sitting quietly in front of electric guitar players,
mariachi bands, women classical saxophonists, avant-garde
jazz ensembles, brothers in do-rags drumming on plastic
buckets and tin cans, a woman playing a saw, an electric
organist playing Guy Lombardo's greatest hits, old Chinese
men playing one-string Chinese violins, Peruvian panpipe
players, young Chinese men playing Chinese flutes, Buddhist
monks playing shakuhachi, doo-wop singers doing close four-
part harmonies, conga players, bongo players, cellists, string
quartets, Hawaiian guitar players, and trombone players, too,
all of them, every one, no matter how good, how bad, it's
music and it's a stay against, an antidote to, the Emperor's
hatred of all that is warm and good and alive. And so the
Subway Philanthropist plies his trade, makes his rounds,
prowls the subways paying one fifty-dollar bill at a time to
keep humanity alive while the Emperor of Death wages war
upstairs, aboveground, in the sad daylight of the world.

He Should Be So Lucky

*One general pulling out a victory
leaves ten thousand corpses to rot.*

TS'AO SUNG

General Hsin Ch'i-chi complains:
*Never the spring wind
will turn this white beard
black again.*

Now, instead of reveling in his book
Destroying Tatars
he's been reduced to reading
How to Plant Trees.

He should be so lucky.
Better he should spend his days
putting young trees into the earth
rather than young bodies.

After the Vision Festival:
New York, New York

Home again in this silent place
hidden on a quiet mountainside
seven hours north of where I was.

Home again to speechless tomatoes,
mute green beans, dumb spinach,
silent cabbages, voiceless potatoes.

No more blare of car horns, sirens,
jackhammers, screech of brakes,
buses pulling away from the curb,

hundreds of people in a room all
talking at once. No more *rumble of
a subway train, rattle of a taxi.*

No more backhoes, pile drivers,
bulldozers, air conditioners, workers
dropping plywood on the sidewalk,

exhaust fans, workers dropping metal
roofing on the sidewalk. Home now and
away from all of that, but home now also

and away from all the music, too. Look.
Ah! listen. See: how music makes sense,
joy, art, ecstasy, out of all that cacophony.

Ode to the Wheelbarrow

No country person or gardener
can exist without it.
A lever with a wheel at one end,
handles on the other,
a bucket of some sort near the wheel,
elegant, useful, simple:
wheelbarrow.

Research says the wheelbarrow
was invented in ancient Greece
about 400 BCE. Could that be?
Something the Chinese
didn't invent?

Don't you wonder who the guy was
who thought to combine the lever
and the wheel?

Imagine your life in the garden
or the yard
without a wheelbarrow.

Summer Blues

You got to understand: here
Winter stays six months a year—
Mean, mean winters and too long.
Ninety days is what we get, just

Ninety days of frost-free weather.
I know you don't believe it but...
Ninety days is all we get. Just
Ninety days of frost-free weather.

And in that lousy, puny, crummy,
Stinkin', measly ninety days we just
Got to get outside and get together!

Now I said, ninety days is all we get.
Just ninety days of frost-free weather
(Believe it, honey, 'cause it's true).
Ninety days is all we get, just

Ninety days of summer weather.
So you can see how we just got to, we
Just got to get outside and get together.

      I said, OUTSIDE! OUTSIDE!
      We got to get OUTSIDE!
      And get together.

And in those ninety days we got to:
Grow tomatoes, beans, potatoes,
Corn, squash, cucumbers, and thyme.

Have barbecues, and a day out on a
Mountain we can climb.

We got to:
Raise some flowers and some pigs,
Build a shed and mow the lawn,
Pick blueberries and mushrooms,
And go skinny-dippin' in the pond.

Got to:
Go to the fair, have sex with warm feet,
Put up a thousand thousand tons of hay,
Go to some dances out of doors,
And cop some rays!

Ow! Ninety days is all we get.
Just ninety days of frost-free weather.
And in that lousy, puny, crummy,
Stinkin', measly ninety days we just
Got to get outside and get together!

  I said, I said, we got to
  Get outside and get together.

And then at night after we been
Skinny-dippin' in the pond
We got to make a campfire
And have a cookout on the lawn.

We got to eat some chicken,
Lie around the fire, drink some wine,
Then watch the night sky let a
Billion, billion stars come out to shine.

I said, OUTSIDE! OUTSIDE!
We just got to get OUTSIDE!
And get together.

At the Open Fire

We all seem to have an innate longing for primitive simplicity, close to the natural state of living.

D.T. SUZUKI, THE ESSENTIALS OF
ZEN BUDDHISM

In the summer sometimes, toward evening, I will build an open fire in the fire pit out beyond the white pine, out by the garden, just in front of the grape arbor. And when I've got a bed of coals, our friends will come out and gather around the fire, spread out blankets on the grass, and we will cook our supper: chicken pieces, lamb and moose kebabs, burgers, salad, potato salad. And while we cook, we'll drink beer and wine and visit with each other. And when the cooking and eating are done, I'll build the fire back up again as darkness falls and the cold air comes spilling down out of the high bog above us.

It's then it happens. I've seen it again and again. Everyone— country folk and city persons alike, it doesn't matter—everyone gathers closer to the fire, and as we continue to visit—although now the talk is quieter—as the stars begin through a clear black sky, all of us stare at the fire. We stare and stare and stare, as if our collective memory were thinking about a time a long time ago.

Respite from the Word

In the beginning was the Word,
and the Word was with God,
and the Word was God.

THE GOSPEL ACCORDING TO JOHN 1:1

Sound of bamboo flute
shakuhachi
wordless notes and tones
pure and clear
impure and unclear
but always wordless
no human voice
running at the mouth
just wordless
notes and tones
just sound

His August Garden

Just last week, or so it seems, the garden
is suddenly middle-aged, tired,
not nubile anymore.

All that lush, young skin, succulent juiciness,
vibrant energy, youthful flexibility:
somehow slipped away.

And in its place: skin beginning to wrinkle,
stalks beginning to harden, everything
becoming brittle, coarse, tired.

Rain after Drought

For two weeks it's been hot and dry—
mercilessly hot and dry—then tonight
in the darkness it began to rain—to
make our vegetables and our hay grow,
to fill our streams, to cool our sweaty
bodies, slake our thirst for water from
the sky. I hear it, I see it, I smell it.
Oh, this blessed, sweet rain.

Somebody's Going to Build a House

Look. Look.   Over there.
Somebody's going to   build a house,
a little house,   a modest house,

something just big enough   for a mother
and a father and a couple of kids.   Two somebodies
are going to build a house.   Two somebodies

are going to start a life.   Two somebodies
are going to have children,   a lawn, a garden,
maybe after a while   put up a garage.

Oh,   it's going to be nice.
A home.   A family.
Even though   in the future

there are going to be   nights
when the adults   can't imagine
staying together   another day,

and maybe even   other nights
years later   after the kids are grown
and gone away   when they

can't imagine   ever being apart.

When

When will I,
like Shōtetsu,
be

too old and tired
for love
or lust?

When will I,
like Shōtetsu,
be

left behind
to watch
those beautiful

young bodies
walk
away?

Forty-Five Years Together

Forty-five years together.
Good times and bad.
In love and out.
Yet always persevering.

Tenacity and grit
are underrated.
Why not praise them, too?

Together to the end.
It is evening.
This is a love poem.

Even After Forty-Five Years

Here in our bedchamber
the heat of our passion
still sets the room aglow.

A Letter from a Friend

The feelings associated with making love,
with all parts of it, from the beginning
to the end, naked flesh pressed against
naked flesh—and coming, too; I don't want
to leave that out—are intense and delicious,

like eating a ripe tomato out of doors
on a summer afternoon,

or walking out on a summer morning
to hear ravens croaking in the dawn or

being awake in the middle of a winter night
sitting alone at the dark table watching
the moon sail across the sky shining white
above the moonlit snow,

these and so many other things
are all so intense and good,

as is, in its quiet way, this letter
that came today from a friend.

How Nice It Is

How nice it is to lie in bed
on a summer night with the windows open
and listen to the thunder far away
and hear the thunder come closer
and see the lightning light up the sky
and then lie in bed in the dark
and listen to the rain.

Part Five

Our Lives Pass Away

Summer sunlight
glitters on the water.

Sweet colors of fall
drift down and land
on my new woodpile.

Winter is full of snow
and cold, but inside
the woodstove glows.

Then spring again.
Our lives pass away.

Melancholy Thought

A bird's path across the sky.
A boat rowing across water.

We are here and gone
without a trace.

What Happened to Me?

When I'm sitting in a chair and I'm wearing shorts
and I cross my left leg over my right and look down
at the skin on the inside of my calf, I see how wrinkled
it is and I realize how old I am and how it is time for me
to understand I'm not a kid anymore, time for me to wrap
my head around my aging life.

What happened to me? I don't know what happened to me.
That skin on the inside of my left calf is a sign to me, a sign
I'm not a young man anymore. What happened to me?
I don't know what happened to me.

Not a Ghost at Peace

Han Shan went to the city and saw young
and beautiful women everywhere. He saw

men, lust bursting from their eyes, trailing
after the women, their tongues hanging out,

like a pack of dogs following a bitch in heat,
all of them thinking only of fucking.

Han Shan says soon those beautiful young women
will be white-haired crones, old and mean and nasty.

Han Shan says so long as men can think of nothing but
the satisfaction of the groin, men will never be free.

Right you are, my friend. Yet I would rather be
trapped here, consumed by lust, than be a ghost at peace.

To the End

I can't leave this mountain. Every time
I leave, I want to come back right away.

CH'E-HUI

I've been here forty years.
I'd like to be here forty more.

The longer I'm here the less
I want to go away, the less

I want to be known. I'd like to
disappear into these mountains,

and never be seen again. I just
want to do my work, make my

poems, and be left alone.
I want to stay here to the end.

Abandoned House

after a poem by Ono no Komachi

Abandoned house on a
mountainside.

Garden gone to
weeds.

Nobody home
anymore.

Praising Myself in the 18th-Century Japanese Style

More arrogant than anyone,
    he refuses
to be anybody's pupil,
    refuses
instruction from any teacher.
    He's just another
bullheaded egomaniac.

He's famous for his gluttony.
    He carries
a basketball around between
    his sternum
and his pelvis.

A bald head, pockmarked face:
    he's a sorry sight.
And all he ever thinks about
    are food and sex.

You'd think a man of seventy
    would know better.

Horizons Far and Near

Why am I so happy here on Judevine Mountain?
My friends say I should travel, see the world.

They say I would improve myself, broaden my
perspectives, expand my horizons. Why can't

they understand I don't want to go anywhere
except out into my woods, down the hill, across

the brook, and up into the stand of big white pine
about half a mile from here.

Here

Here
right next to me
an old pine
leaning
with the weight of years
holds on
a little longer.

Then and Now

In Yang Wan-li's China 800 years ago,
Yang went from place to place by boat,
across lakes, up and down the Yangtze.

Imagine: never able to travel faster than
the river current. Day after day, all that
time to read, play a flute, watch the mist

rising between mountains as you float by.
Toward evening: an inn, dinner, sleep,
up the next day and back again to the boat.

Imagine those slow days:
all that time to read, write, watch, dream
while you float toward tomorrow.

In an Instant

after Yang Wan-li

The place where I
stopped last night
is far away today.

Tomorrow,
tonight
will be last night.

In an instant,
the present
is the past.

I was a kid
just yesterday, today
I'm an old man.

In the Little Notebook I Carry in My Overalls

For two hours I've been out in the woods,
dropping trees, cutting trunks and branches
into 16-inch lengths and stacking brush. Now

I'm stretched out on the fallen white pine
needles, lycopodium, yellow maple leaves,
drinking water, resting, looking at the sky.

After a while I take the pen and little notebook
from the pocket high up on the left-hand side
of my overalls and write down an early version

of this poem. Then I put the pen and notebook
back, stretch out again, hands behind my head:
Watch. Listen. Mid-October morning. Fifty degrees.

Almost all the leaves are down. No sound.
No breeze. Only now and then a flock of geese
going over, high and far away.

Out in the Fall Woods

Out in the fall woods again this year,
    cutting firewood.

Now sitting under a big white pine tree
    writing this,

I wonder how many more years
    I will be able to

work here, wander here,
    do this:

smell the dying ferns
    and leaves, listen to

the geese going south, stare up through
    the branches of

these trees, see the clear-blue-blue-clear
    autumn sky.

Still Here

Still out here in the woods dropping trees,
bucking firewood, using a chain saw all
alone and at my age too. People say
I should stop before I kill myself.

They say I'm too old for this. Here's
what Yuan Mei said 250 years ago:
Of course I know I'm going to die.
I also know I'm not dead yet.

I Love My Aging Self This Way

All day I've hauled wood
into the woodshed and
stacked it row after neat
row. Why is this simple
chore so satisfying? It's
cold now, cloudy, gray.
The trees full of color.
Geese go over all day.

Inside: Evening:
My chest and arms,
legs and back all ache
so much I can barely
move. The whiskey is
a great relief. We eat
a simple meal of kale,
newly dug potatoes,
shell beans. In spite
of everything, I love
my aging self this way.

Another Fall

Withered garden plants heaped upon the compost pile,
garden tilled and smooth and resting, woodshed full,
air cold, sky clear, mountains red and yellow.

How many more times to see this turning from life to death?
How much longer to be healthy and want to be a part of this?
When will my own turning toward death make me look—

as my father looked at the end—only inward so that I
can't see what's out there, beyond me, in this sweet world?

Tumbling Toward the End

Finally we have enough money,
even in these difficult times,
if we are careful how we spend it.

What's to worry about?
One child is dead, the other grown.
We're tumbling toward the end.

Happy Life

At my desk all morning.
In the woods all afternoon.
Headed home now through the yellow light.

Yang Wan-li said,
There's enough to eat.
Who needs a lot of money?

I've led a happy life
doing what I want to do.
How could I be so lucky?

After Looking at Wu Zhen's *Fisherman*

Wu Zhen lived the life of a recluse.
He never was very famous or successful.

His drawing shows a cartoonlike
simplicity and directness.

He was the hermit-fisherman, the symbol
in the late Yuan period of the unemployed scholar.

He stirs his oar, puts aside his fishing pole,
and floats toward evening.

About the Author

David Budbill's previous two books of poems are *While We've Still Got Feet* (2005) and *Moment to Moment: Poems of a Mountain Recluse* (1999), both from Copper Canyon Press. Garrison Keillor reads frequently from David's poems on NPR's *The Writer's Almanac*.

In 1999, Chelsea Green Publishing released a revised, expanded version of *Judevine*, his collected poems.

Judevine, the play, has now had 65 productions in 22 states since the early 1980s. Among Budbill's other plays are *Little Acts of Kindness, Thingy World!, Two for Christmas*, and his newest, *A Song for My Father*, which received two separate productions in 2010.

In January 2009 David received his first Honorary Doctor of Humane Letters from New England College, Henniker, New Hampshire.

He lives in the mountains of northern Vermont with his wife, the painter Lois Eby, and there he writes, cuts firewood, gardens, and plays bamboo flutes.

His website is at www.davidbudbill.com.

Since 1972, Copper Canyon Press has fostered the work of emerging, established, and world-renowned poets for an expanding audience. The Press thrives with the generous patronage of readers, writers, booksellers, librarians, teachers, students, and funders — everyone who shares the belief that poetry is vital to language and living.

Copper Canyon Press gratefully acknowledges board member

JIM WICKWIRE

for his many years of service to poetry and independent publishing.

MAJOR SUPPORT HAS BEEN PROVIDED BY:

WASHINGTON STATE
ARTS COMMISSION

The Paul G. Allen Family Foundation

Amazon.com

Anonymous

Diana and Jay Broze

Beroz Ferrell & The Point, LLC

Golden Lasso, LLC

Gull Industries, Inc.
on behalf of William and Ruth True

Lannan Foundation

Rhoady and Jeanne Marie Lee

National Endowment for the Arts

Cynthia Lovelace Sears and Frank Buxton

Washington State Arts Commission

Charles and Barbara Wright

To learn more about underwriting
Copper Canyon Press titles, please call
360-385-4925 X103

The Chinese character for poetry is made up of two parts: "word" and "temple." It also serves as pressmark for Copper Canyon Press.

This book is set in Minion, designed for digital composition by Robert Slimbach in 1989. Minion is a neohumanist face, a contemporary typeface retaining elements of the pen-drawn letterforms developed during the Renaissance. Display type is set in Woodland, designed by Akira Kobayashi. Book design and composition by Valerie Brewster, Scribe Typography. Printed on archival-quality paper at McNaughton & Gunn, Inc.